run

wild

and

be

run wild and be

Poems & short stories
Inspired by endurance running & wild spaces

sydney
zester

ISBN 9781798405703

All photos by Sydney Zester unless otherwise noted.
Book design by Script and Vine

KDP, 2019

www.runwildandbe.com

a love letter

to young me,
sweet girl live for yourself

to the run,
my freedom

to him,
my steady and gentle love

to us
you & she & her & we

CONTENTS

run wild & be

———

MOMENTS MOVING

———

DAY 1 TRAIL NOTES

/////

The humidity is hanging low, heavy and moist; every stride feels like a thick plod through murky water. Sweat trickles from my pores like a forgotten faucet left to run into waste. And yet, here I am pushing up a hill and feeling utterly nothing. Well, nothing of the heat or the humidity or the gnats smacking my neck and face, making home on my damp skin. But inside--oh inside. There's a bite in the fullest part of stomach. Rooted in core with vines wrapping around my womanhood and heart and up through my veins. It's trying to claw up into my throat; a shrill scream sits at my tonsils patiently waiting for my mouth to grow tired and weakly fall open so it can escape, wild and unhinged. Yes well this is something I'm acutely aware of. Not the gnats or the heat or the dull ache in my quads.

And yet my body keeps moving.

The song playing on my ipod stops and then there's just silence; but something else too. I can't place that noise. I wonder to myself, as a fly down the hill, where that dull buzz could be stemming from. Unable to hold my attention, my mind drifts away from the noise and towards my surroundings.

The river is flowing next to me, the water line is high, hinting to all the late summer storms we'd been having the past

3

couple weeks. There were only a few trucks parked along the road, tire tracks chiseled deep in the fresh mud, showing some folks decided to brave the heat for some fishing.

I start to imagine people floating silently on the water doing whatever you do when you fish. Maybe thinking? Or reading? Maybe talking to the fish and the birds? Honestly, I don't fish. I cannot begin to fathom what you are supposed to do with all that idle time. I have to keep moving, that's why I run and don't fish, I silently confirm to myself.

I keep moving forward. There is no breeze, just a heavy swath of green. As if someone took a paint can, dumped along the river and lazily swashed a brush over it. The trees look full and healthy. I look at it and keep going, not really noticing anything in particular. Just running and moving and going. Totally unaware of pace or fatigue.

As I wind around the bend and begin the steep ascent, pushing off my toes and lightly swinging my arms, I bring my attention back to that unidentifiable noise I noticed earlier. It is still there buzzing in the silence. For the life of me I cannot place it. I fuddle around with my earphones, wondering for a moment if maybe they had gone wonky, but nothing changed.
The road is uneven here and I move to my right to stay clear of the sharp edge. I am still ascending the climb and my hamstrings have started to burn. My consciousness draws in, my breathing has become incredibly labored, something that really shouldn't happen on this one familiar road. I suddenly realize that sound was me.

And then it clicks, I've been crying. Probably for a while, maybe not. Tears quickly running straight down my face.

The only thing consuming me, eating at my stomach in that painful way anxiety does, was that he had gone and now there was fear. All the fear I had been pushing aside for the past year had come to fruition and was insisting it would not be ignored. Manifesting physically while my brain still tried to numbly inch away from it. And yet that was impossible. I knew what had happened and I had no clue what was to come. Complete fear of whether we would fall out of love or love someone else or just the missing him would never go away.

I didn't know what would be worse: losing him or missing him.

This question had sat inside my body and brain since we began writing applications. Intent on not being "that couple", we tried to pursue schools that filled us up as individuals and offered a wide range of course work. Our financial situations were vastly different and so that played a big part in final choice; I had spent months anxiously waiting to see if I qualified for any scholarships or aide, something he didn't have to worry about. Where we finally landed had felt manageable in the hypothetical. We were only a few cities apart, there were trains we could take, and ultimately we thought we were making the best decision for ourselves.

But that thought process was all hanging in space, controlled for time and distance and fullness of schedules. There was never an actual experience of being apart for extended time and understanding what that would be like. There wasn't talk of how short visits would feel or how stunting it would be when he left. I was realizing now, that in my effort to manage my anxiety and face this new chapter as it came, I also was wildly unprepared for the change. This was made evident by the near panic attack I was experiencing as I mindlessly ran up and down my backroads.

I turned my iPod back on to that same song but it wasn't really resonating. It sort of just hummed in the background while I wiped tears and sweat and sunscreen from my eyes. That burning combination paled in comparison to the tear in my belly.

run wild & be

7

pace slow, run fast

she practices pacing
each morning when
she moves slowly enough
to sleepily sip coffee
while the sun slips through
the old window pane

always

sometimes it's really good
to feel little and bare
and breathe in pine stained air.

snow day run

wiggle on your wool socks
and pull on your puffy
then quietly just start and go
because we all know
later can quickly turn to never
if you don't take the first
few steps, out in the snow

run wild & be

two weeks before the taper

feeling sleepy like a
river bed run dry

killarney lessons

chaos can be calm
like running down new roads
when the alternative is
growing stale
I'd rather grow wild.

nourish

crisp apples & air
mud caked ankles
boxed wine & summits

lincoln logs

today's run
flow did not come
no spirit from
my skull seeping
down to my
pattering feet
instead
twill fibers of my muscles
broke and built
like the wood
for a log cabin

run wild & be

peak weeks

shirt tucked in tights
for double run day
so now up and go
fill up your cup
and water your roots

small moments

she parks her car, steps out,
and stretches for a moment
letting the pine air hit her
and wake her up. She starts
down through town, passing
the coffee shop she'll end at,
letting herself briefly imagine
the hot, chocolatey dark roast
she'll enjoy when she works
her way back down the mountain.
for now, she hangs a left and
starts pushing up and up and up.
out of town and to the trailhead.

magic/flow

magic trickles every time
she didn't want to go
but went outside anyway
and ended up feeling
her skin shiver and sparkle,
not from the chill,
but from reaching flow

finally full

running between the pines and
the peppermint in the air
pulls a tear down her face

run wild & be

free

wild moments
spent leaning
into herself

hill repeats & recover

some days we bundle up
and run hill repeats outside
in the hollow winter air.
other days we wrap up cozy
and slurp mugs of coffee
while snug on the sofa.
i think it's best to do both.

training plan

today i turned a
dreamy dream
into a lofty goal
and am learning
to trust that my body
will carry me there

endurance

the run
will break
your body
and build
your soul

long run progression

long turns
to short
before dream
can turn
to memory

autumn miles

dead leaves falling
from tired trees
breathes her energy

run wild & be

grad school

cold runs on old city streets

slower intentions

waking up with wildflowers in
skinny alpine air.
coffee mornings sipping
outside and in bed.
dusk runs that go into dark.
evenings at home with the
windows open
and scratch made pasta sauce
simmering.
running fast to feel wild &
alive
on-a-whim road trips to do her
long run next
to the ocean with salty air
spraying her skin
& smiling when she tracks
sand into the car

two medicine

sharp and soft
your peaks
whisper quietly,
a snow stained
breeze drips through
my sweat drenched t-shirt,
and lions mane
more like a waterfall.
now, take a minute to
lean in and let the world
make you feel small.

summer to fall

marathon training
happy making
pizza eating
sleep.

training grind

excitement is helpful,
hard work is required,
but time tends to operate
independently of our
wants and desires.
we can be overflowing
with happiness and hardness
and yet improvements are
bound to time.
they peak out when
time says "ok, go ahead".

grinnel

throbbing thick thighs
sweat slipping down my spine
each breath blasting through my ear drums
climbing me from the base to the peak
more religion than the stained glass
will bring

first few miles

when she passes the nagging
wonder in her mind asking when
she should turn around or
maybe should she slow down,
she is finally free.

night run

snow-smell hung in the air
and my breath colored
the space in front of me
brain bouncing feet over
the cracking city
magical twinkling orbs brim
from the trees and transform
the night, while i run
through the streets

twitchy

every night
sleep slips away
from my mind.
thoughts race,
like my legs love to.
'you make us so happy'
mind says to feet,
'let me try.'

run wild & be

rest day

rain on a
tin roof
kind of
sunday

run wild & be

last miles of a long run

flurries dust her jacket like
a sprinkle of powdered sugar
on saturday morning pancakes

run wild & be

stained brain

tent flies
sugar coat
her daydreams

goals / dreams / trees for company

when she wakes up
she'll slip on her hokas,
walk outside, stand for a
moment on the porch
& let the freeze pinch her
nose & catch her breath
then she'll just simply
take off and go
because she knows,
not to sit and wait
that early in the morning,
motivation is never awake

gump

she just felt like running
like forrest or in the forest
it didn't matter

true love

the run
made space
in her heart,
sat down &
never left

run wild & be

real glam

workout wednesday //
hard effort coughs
snot covered sleeves
crusty, sleepy eyes &
grit covered dreams

run wild & be

when life imitates the run

big //
hills
quads
dreams
loaves

41

———

PEOPLE & PEAKS

———

ZION TRAIL NOTES

////

The peacefulness is almost overwhelming. So is the canyon. So is the pain in my Achilles--it's snaking up the back of my ankle and shooting into the pain part of my brain, refusing to be ignored. It's just after sunrise and the light of the sun is starting to give the canyon a bit of life. Shadows fade and we are welcomed with vibrant paint strokes of red and orange everywhere we look. Off in the distance you can see three little dots--humans--bob up and down, running with the early morning glitter.

A few miles into our run I switch training groups, Jen was feeling sharp pain and wanted to press on but we talked about it and decided she really shouldn't ignore her body. So I joined up with Matt and Zach. I'm thankful to be running with the boys instead of Jen—she was a little too chatty for 6 AM, which really feels like 5am since we crossed into Mountain time yesterday. Unfortunately, sticking with the boys also means running at a clip that hovers just one step out of reach. I can absolutely keep up (my ego wouldn't allow anything else) and I'm thankful to have underestimated my speed all these years, but dang it certainly isn't a relaxing pace. The dudes are chatting and laughing a bit, kindly trying to engage me as well. I open my mouth to respond and all I can muster is a little spit and a labored groan. Matt smiles at me, gives me the sign 4KOK, and turns back to Zach.

Over the past few weeks I had devised a plan for when I was paired with the super-speedy crowd. Over and over again I repeated "push push push push". I didn't let my mind wander and didn't lose focus, it was an act of mental toughness I was beginning to welcome openly. Running always felt meditative to me but this new trick was awakening a different part of me.

As we silently pace closer to Zion's entrance, things around us get a bit more interesting. The llamas in the few yards we pass look just as confused to see us as we are to see them. Houses are few and far between. For a quick moment I let myself wonder who lives in the llama houses. What does their normal look like? Where do they buy groceries? What do they do for a living? I draw my attention back to my teammates who are now easily 4 or 5 strides ahead. "Push push push push pushhhhhhh" I catch up to the back of the group, feeling like I may have used the last ounce of energy I had.

The boys and I continue to sway up and down the climbs— we've fallen into a relaxing rhythm. My Achilles still hurts. The canyon walls engulf us, towering over as a humble reminder where we lie on the Earth. How many people had passed this canyon wall in its entire existence? I wonder to myself. I felt small.

Zack starts talking about his mama—a fighter and survivor. I stop thinking about my Achilles.

We pass a sign for a town limit. Population: 18. Huh. That's smaller than our team and we fit into two 15 passenger vans. We see the van off in the distance. Although out here even when we see it, we're still a good mile and a half out from it. Just like time, distance and space mean so little to me now. I don't really mind though—it's cool today, a nice breeze whispers through the canyon and across my skin. The closest tangible thing to peace besides our daily 5am gas station coffee.

Truthfully, my body is tanked from yesterday's 13 miles through the Mojave Desert at high noon. And this morning we were welcomed with a time change; we all groggily bid that extra hour farewell. But still, I literally wouldn't trade it for the world. I'm totally in love with life in this moment. Exhausted, un-showered, hungry and all. We run the last three miles to Zion's gates, all together.

run wild & be

8 words say it all

the 4000 mile run that carried me home

role models

it was a mystical mixing
where strangers became sisters,
where i learned living and loving
no longer wanted to cohabitate,
where goals grew from
his sparkling blue eyes to the
glittering snow-capped peaks,
of everywhere else.

purple mountain majesty

the first time i met you
your skinny air
clenched my lungs.
it didn't matter though
i looked at you and learned
what it felt like to be free
and that had already stolen
my breath away

ocean to ocean

if you would like to get to know
your most intimate self
set out to run ocean to ocean,
you will be surprised what you learn
in the rockies

growing pains

each day the pain in my tendons grew
leading me to wonder if running back to you
was my achilles heel

reflection

while she runs
wild & free & sleepy
she wonders quietly
what would her body be
if she drew a self-portrait.
maybe, an evergreen tree
and her hair would be
pine needles that
whisper in her ears with
every soft breeze
her feet you wouldn't
even be able to see,
she decides,
since she is so speedy

monterey

day one was run
with pebble beach
to the right and
cherry stands off
to the left and
your ashes drifting
across the green

highway 1

sweet sur, you were the launching pad
to the childlike wonder and surrender,
to the indescribable.
a plod along your cliffs, through fields
of zippy wildflowers and reckless poison oak
that stung my skin and my hippocampus
burning into the memory of your salt drenched air.

barstow

one dusty road
down the desert
with a bull in a cage
hidden in the canyons
the air was eerie
running on the
ghost road route
littered with white crosses.
the miles filled our
feet with flames
and our hearts with
memories of lives
lost too soon

mojave

we started at the firehouse and slowly inched
out of the city confines towards the
beckoning orange canyons, anxious energy was
quickly replaced by repetitive thoughts
left right left right left right
all to conserve energy. We were beat down
running one mile at a time before bringing our
body temperature back down in the van
but when we finished I knew I fought hard for you.

pocatello

the moments were filled
with fifteen miles
through the idaho openness
and the horses curiously
watched us while we
had a dance party on the side
of the road to celebrate
another day conquered

jackson hole

snow smell hung low
and pine needles puddled
on the soft soil
like a freshly made bed
though, I was too sleepy to
have a spiritual experience

thoughts in kentucky

body, self
i am sorry.
you house me
carry me
run me.
you change every day,
showing me
it's possible.
so i'm sorry
i valued you
only on
six small crevices
a pack of six

cross country

we ran for those who can't
but now i can see
I also ran for me
the me who wanted identity
outside of B

dirtbag glamorous

gas station coffee
sleeping on fire
station floors and
pooping in the desert

run wild & be

sweet cakes

my sisters heart was as sweet
as her face was round

nomadic

the hard part wasn't the nights
spent sleeping on the church floors
or the brain breaking down behaviors
so ingrained it feels like skin shedding.

the hard part was not to lose it all, once
back to what was normal before.

grow slow

i felt like a tree in the summer
with a secret no one knew
while I was gone,
all my colors changed
dropped to the ground
and grew back new.
but people saw and
thought it was the old you.
4000 miles of rockies,
deserts, yellow & blue
lay hidden beneath the green
& in the old running shoe

slow start

MILE 1
//
clunky quads
crusty eyes
cold fingers
coffee.

MILE 9
//
thinking about
eggs and toast
but wish i had
time for one
more mile

everyday

the moments when awe & evergreen
slowly shut my mouth because
any sound slipped would shatter
the trance and smudge the memory

slow intentions

waking up with wildflowers in skinny alpine air
coffee mornings spent sipping outside or in bed
dusk runs that go into dark
evenings at home with the windows open
and scratch-made pasta sauce simmering
running fast to feel wild and free
on-a-whim road trips to do her long run next
to the ocean, with salty air spraying her skin
& smiling when she tracks sand into the car

mike

every blister,
pained muscle,
burnt inch of skin
was my chance
to honor you

early morning legs

sun rises
and she
does too.
slips on
each shoe
rubs one eye
then two.

run wild & be

4K

the people and peaks
add a face and shape
to my heart

fresh air / hard work / chocolate

have you figured out the concoction
that enchants your dizzy drunk brain
so wildly & madly in love with your life

4000 miles

she loved running
across her country
-coast to coast-
so much so that
now those 4000 miles
have made a home
snug in her cells

intimate partner

that impossible to ignore
tug, deep in her core
that pulls the car to a
halt when she's driving
down an empty road,
swallowed by evergreens.
she steps out and inhales
the peppermint air, then
simply starts running
straight ahead, towards
the sitting summit. warm
tingles trace down her skin
and cracked across
her face, a toothy grin.
perhaps this is a clue
that our bodies know
freedom far more
intimately than
our minds do.

first fourteener

she grabbed her sleeping bag
stuffed it into a pack &
ran long up the peak
then when she was done,
wrapped herself in the puff
& rested her legs in the
ice blue alpine lake

———

LONG DISTANCE

run/love

———

GLACIER TRAIL NOTES

////

I walk to the edge of the road, gravel crunching under my Hokas and a slight evergreen stained breeze dusting my face. Goosebumps run down my spine, not out of chill but fascination. My only decision was turn left or right. I turn right. Immediately I start pushing up the hill, my legs turning over much quicker than they normally would. We had been in the car close to the entire day. We woke up in Cracker Barrel parking lot after a restless night, stumbled in for some sweet golden nectar and then got back on the road. Stress was a building most of the day. He and I were just not mushing right today. It was upsetting and confusing because I couldn't pinpoint why.

I'm now a half mile down the road, feet bouncing below me, Lake McDonald to my right. I feel alive. The trees smell like home and the whisper slipping between their branches twinkles through my mind. Finally it feels like my racing mind begins to slow. My panic about us subsides and my determination to simply love with no expectations returns. I think about him setting up the tent back at camp. Probably still agitated over our argument. What was it about? I can't remember anymore. Tuna fish? Was it maybe about eating tuna fish for dinner? It feels far, far away now. Now it's just me and the trees and the mountains.

I wonder if I should turn around soon. My attention moves from the peak to the bear spray clutched in my left hand. I was still new at this. Grizzlies and I don't know each other very well. And I really didn't know what I'd do if I saw one.

"HI BEAR." I blurted out, a little spit spraying from my lips. Unsure if that did anything helpful and feeling admittedly a little stupid. "HI BEAR" almost like a convulsion another bursts from my lips. This was probably safe, I thought.

I keep pushing up. The smell is just too good. I know I'll be able to smell the firey evergreens when I'm back at camp but it's not going to be the same. It won't be like this. Peace in movement and lost in thought with a wide open heart. I continued to run. Up and up and up.

At the gates of Glacier, I cried. This place slept in my heart for a very long time, and now we were meeting for the first time. It was overwhelming. We also had run out of food, had no plans for what to eat for dinner, it started pouring as soon as we drove in.

"HI BEAR." Over and over I'm spilling this line. It starts to pair with my stride which is a little fun. I feel like a human metronome. I was probably a spectacle if someone saw me, just there was no one out there. Just me the peaks and the grizzlies.

real love

miss you less than
the regret stings
when I mumble
I'm not ready
for you to grow

long distance

happy, happy fleeting.
i search for it in your
voice, but still
nothing musters.
no tingle or crackle.
the trees, the road
and hollow crisp air,
my sore, sleepy legs
try to tell me.
stop seeking it
in him but instead
lean into me.

grow up

you're cold and eerie
i'm sore and sleepy
you stay stuck
because your concrete roots
i hope no one can
say that about me

her hollow

even magical hot springs
on bitter cold days
cannot warm the hollow
in her core
she now lovingly
calls hers

growing pains

our big bang started in september
when i came home to find
all our parts no longer fit together.
the boom shoved distance into our
simple adoration and now we got to
sit and stare at a stranger in a sweatshirt
that smelled familiar.

run wild & be

crave

small moments
in big spaces

f word

fortitude is four years fighting
because you're apart but wish you weren't
and when missing turns to anger
you stay there anyway because
you promised him forever

panic attack v. 1

every day was damning
but chaos finally won
and clenched to her lungs

maryland

we talk until we're blue
and all the words are spoken.
so why don't i feel better
why can't i tell you forever

north carolina

i'm supposed to treasure
and love
and cherish
and praise
you.
but i don't
even know you

run wild & be

heart health

she runs so long
to forget the pain
of being
so far
from you

motivation

every day
i will try to
run the distance
that sits between us
and maybe i will feel
closer to you.

self-inflicted

your only responsibility
is to love wholly
and honor your insides.
as soon as we start making
decisions for others, we step
into an endlessly unfulfillable space
and begin to break our own hearts.

don't cross off days

how about
instead of
counting down
we just sit
within the
slipping moments

a poem inside a promise

while yes, we've only ever loved each other
sometimes our partnership has felt like many.
fractured moments and points in time.
i've broken your heart and you have mine.

actions

people who preach grace
rarely practice it

year nine lessons

no amount of discomfort is ever
a lighter load to carry
than the weight of regret
we feel from holding
the other back.

little one

needing you
crushed me
so never again
will i naively
drink the narrative
to need is to love

sligo

they'd been together so long
she sometimes lost her end
and his begin
so she flew across the atlantic
to run down irish roads
and up gaelic mountains
tracing her ancestors' footsteps
looking to know
if he goes & she's left sitting
quiet and alone, could she
still be happy as me

dusk

she saw pink skies
and ran through
her blue heart

high school sweetheart

sometimes I would go run
where we first became one
and when I was finished
i'd take off my shoes
and step my bare feet on
the soft bermuda grass
my lungs burning like before
and ears stinging
I would just stand and wonder
how we got so far from
days of field hockey and football

———

RUN/HER

———

IRELAND TRAIL NOTES

/////

I take a sip of my coffee, saying a thankful prayer for the 10th time that morning for finally finding a coffee shop. I had woken up with an insane migraine and slipped out of my AirBnB, trying to intuitively navigate Sligo and find city center. When I finally stumbled this small bakery squished between a pub and a cathedral I squealed out loud.

It was a beautiful city. The cobblestone roads and colored row homes. People were nice but not over the top. It felt working class and had a charming air about it. So much made me feel like I was home. Even though an ocean separated me from my Baltimore, I felt connected to the space. When I was searching for my coffee I found myself constantly wondering if my great grandfather had walked here. What it looked like when he did.

I gulped down the last drips of my coffee. And decided that it was time to head out. There was a huge day of miles and adventure to be had! I slowly walk out of the warm comfort of the bakery, smiling bye to the sweet gals behind the counter, and step out onto the cobblestone street. It's a busy morning, people are rushing around to work and school. It makes me feel comfortable, seeing everyone live their normal lives; this certainly was not a tourist town. I felt like I could blend in a bit more that way. I start walking out of city center--the roads feel too busy to start running yet. Plus I can already tell I tied my shoes too tight. I'll stop to loosen them when I get to the last of the row homes.

I meander through the skinny roads, passing by person after person while peering into the little shops. The river runs by me down at the bottom of the hill and a few people are standing there watching it flow. How oddly normal this felt. I reach the one intersection and wait for my turn to cross, the green and red row homes welcoming me on the other side. I bend over to loosen my shoes and take a minute to enjoy that stretch. Even after that sleep and all the coffee, I still feel a bit zonked. Knowing this feeling all too well, the only way to start is just to do it. Turn off the brain and just start moving my legs. And so I go. Balancing on the narrow walkway next to the main road. A sign tells me it will take me to the coast. And so I keep heading west.

My legs felt really heavy but I focused on everything around me and calming down from that email. I still hadn't spoke to Brian yet. This first part of the run was exactly how I imagined running in Ireland--green farms, sheep, farm houses, mountain views, and skinny roads.

I took the first left off the main drag and paced past a community park. It reminded me of home except there was actually someone using the exercise structures. I got to the end of the road and felt like I should turn right. I studied the map a bit last night and had at least a little bit of intuition to pull me towards the coast. Pulling out my phone to double check, I looked to see if he had woken up yet. He hadn't; no missed calls. But I was happy to see my intuition wasn't wrong. Tossing my phone back into my pack to turned right and started plodding down the road. Skinny and surrounded by green, it felt just like I had hoped. The gray sky hadn't opened up yet and just lingered above, a constant reminder that I certainly was not in the southern US anymore.

I passed small cottage after small cottage. Then a large, old farm house with rusted equipment and sheep scattered around the surrounding fields. I wondered what the people's lives were like who lived here. If anyone liked to go for runs on these roads.

A hushed chug of an engine drew my attention in. I quickly stepped to the side of the road to let the car pass. My mind rushed with quick anxiety--my biggest fear was being hit by a car while I was running here because I would step to the wrong side of the road. It had been quiet enough so far that I was feeling a little bit more at ease but there was a rush of prickles down my skin every time I heard something. "You need to calm down, jeez Syd" I muttered to myself.

The winding road proved to have far more incline than I had thought a coastal space would. I guess running towards a mountain has something to do with it, I sarcastically think to myself. My brain feels all over the place. I chalk it up to the long travel and the bad news email. And traveling abroad for the first time by myself. I need to give myself way more credit.
The road is getting steeper and steeper and the houses are getting scarcer. The cows, however, have grown in abundance and seem to be maybe just a smidge interested in me. At least they look over towards me when I run past.

It feels like the turn for the trail up to the mountain should be near. Knocknarea is within view and growing larger with every stride towards her. Knowing there was an ancient burial ground at the summit gave me mixed feelings. In one breath, I was thrilled that I could be traveling the same spaces my great grandfather had, most likely by foot too. On the other hand, I was curious to see how I would feel at the summit. I had done very rudimentary research on my family history prior to coming over. I knew we had been farmers-- just common folk--and had trickled slowly over to the United States. I researched little with intention. I wondered how I would feel running where my ancestors lived, walked, worked, and died. I wanted very little to haze my intuition while I spent time here.

The ground beneath me was becoming rocky and wet. The pavement had ended and I was officially making my way up to the base of the mountain. I probably wouldn't call what I was doing "running" at this point. More power hiking/trying not to slip, break an ankle in a foreign country, and have to navigate my way through an unknown medical system. I momentarily look up from the spot three steps ahead of me and find myself looking squarely at a collection of bright turquoise antique tractors. Their presence almost felt like a punch in the eyes up against the foggy, wet landscape. I take a photo of them and decide to keep moving forward. Up ahead, I see a few cars parked by a map nailed to a wooden board. Knowing I'm where I should be gives me a boost to bound up the mountain.

I'm moving quickly but still not technically running. My eyes are glued in front of me, hands braced on my quads for support and brain is just repeating "move up move up move up" over and over again. Suddenly, I feel the pressure weaken, my labored breathing calms and I look up. In front of me is a large mound of rocks. Probably as big as a few houses stacked on top of each other and placed next to each other. "Did I make it?" I wonder aloud. No one is around so I'm simply talking to the air.

I walk towards the massive structure and see a small sign. Written on it, in simple lettering, a request that all visitors respect the space that this is--an ancient burial ground--and not touch or climb on anything.

Wow. I take a minute to see how I feel. I try to calm my brain and my body to connect with the space. My mind continues to race. I'm feeling nothing much so far which is disappointing. Maybe I need to keep moving to a different space, i resolve with myself. So, slowly through the deep mud, I start running around the space. Eyes never leaving it, feet constantly sinking too far into the ground. Just as i feel my sleep deprived, lonely, frustration start to boil into what would surely be a moment of weakness, i see it. I smell it.

The Atlantic. I'm on a cliff that sits above a small town, the homes sprinkled below me, and then the massive blue ocean wrapping around every curve, divot, and line. It feels like a hug. A beautiful, familiar hug.

"HELLO! I know you!!" I scream with delight. Immediately, peace and awe replace my frustration.

I don't know what to do. I feel everything all at once. If I keep moving forward this moment will be over and gone. If I stay where I am I won't be able to touch the ocean. My sinking feet encourage me to at least move forward to a dryer spot.

I feel like a child. Free and wild. Overwhelmed with happiness and completely in awe of what I am able to do in this moment.

girl, don't grow weary

it gets tiring
pacing fight or flight
with left and right

gal pals

together sweet girl
we'll be free
of the young man's need
and his fragile ego.
we will exist together
twinkling and full
outside the system
created for the white-him
sustained by hate and power.

unending thanks

she who came before me
who couldn't run wild & free
who had to hide under
a hat and baggy hoodie
because of she i can be
me, and run openly
through fields &
wild streets & busy roads.
her heart and fight
pushed aside the angry he's
so i can pace down the street
with a little paper pinned
to my damp tee
without anyone yelling
about my ovaries

for future reference

loving unconditionally
comes without
strings attached
to honor

peachy keen

tempo tuesday
ended tingly
knowing she
added another
run to the
goal bucket

run wild & be

workout day things

baby hairs,
snot rockets &
"i think i cans"

grounded

her body, strong and seeped in sweat,
reaching for release and rundown
with the last of the miles,
breathes out as the river
trickles next to her.

run wild & be

but you didn't get the license plate

she was once out
for a run & followed
by a man with knife
around and around
the river until she
could finally get
away and tell the
police who looked
at her with bored,
uninterested
disposition

girl code

girl, you deserve to be
loved unconditionally:
to have consensual,
mind-blowing sex as
frequently as you feel.
to run as far and fast
as you can, without
being yelled at by a man.
to say no to plans
because you'll be
home sitting quietly
in your stretchy pants.
you can take their name
or keep your own,
that decision stays
sacred in your home.
just remember, when
we make decisions to
comfort others, we step
into an endlessly unfulfillable
space & begin to break
our own hearts.

city roads

my braid is not
an invitation
to approach
and grope
not a leverage point
to snake, pull, and yank
my shape, my body
is not an automatic pass go
No.
my power is not diminished
by your present manhood
No.
my power, like a peak
strong, unfazed by your
little fleeting footsteps
though each towards me
still, too close for comfort

opinions are like butts

maybe if you loved more
and judged less
your own pain
could evaporate

honks & spit & yells & grabs

fear sometimes whispers
"staying inside would be easier"
but thanks to anger & righteousness
she's run some of her
speediest splits
-outside-

a resolve, or perhaps more, a promise

to know that i control me,
not them, him, or he
to undo the conditioning that
says i can buy a better me.
to run long because
it makes me feel free.
to love unconditionally on the
heart who knows every inch of me
to believe that my prayers may
look different than theirs
but an all loving God doesn't
prescribe to man-made laws.
to anticipate judgment without
fear and still live wildly
because 2018 taught me,
when i live for he or she
emptiness creeps into a vibrant heart,
slowly and wholly.
so let this be the year
we simply run wild & be

real apex predator

isn't it odd to think
that a man in a truck
on quiet back roads
drums up more fear
than a bear out
on an empty trail

firewood bundled dreams

when her ears start burning
and she's a little sleepy & sore
goals keep her going until
she can't run anymore

run like a girl

after swiveling around in her chair,
pausing to boil a pot of tea, then
meticulously melting the honey-
finally pressing purchase on her
spring marathon, she decided, was
really her confirming to herself
that she believes she has power
to grow / change / make gains

mountain/muse

flowers freckled across the field,
as her heart raced up the hillside,
little dribbles of water leaked from
her pack and dripped down her back.
both legs trying to turnover to pace
towards the craggy, haunting peak

the occasional butt wrinkle

dear me / body
i love you.
your curves, cracks
crevices & cartilage
carry me, run me
house & home me.
all you ask for in return
is for me to consume
lots of water & veggies
and for me to stop
mumbling ew gross
when i see a mark that
says i lived my life

if only we had the same dad

my sister
is the
only mate
my soul
seeks

her freedom

every single mile doesn't have
to be run hard up a hillside &
every single meal doesn't need
to be painstakingly planned

run / her flow

on today's tempo run
one flow did not come
but her cycle circled back
and every step felt clumsy &
heavy. so she ended with a
heating pad on her belly,
hot tea with honey in her
hands & a gentle reminder
that this is her gal power

marathon / life / road

in a field of white men
be a strong, brave woman

run wild & be

her honor

because of all the shes
that came before me
i get to run wild & be

126

rituals

she tugs up
her lion mane
into a messy bun
& then head knows
it's time to run

———

FULL

———

OLYMPIC TRAIL NOTES

/////

I stare at the sign hanging in front of us. In big bold letters "Cougar Country" written across the paper, the layers of dirt hint to the age of posting. No matter, I scan the steep cliffs above us, peering through the dusk shadows wondering if there's anyone watching us. I try not to think too hard about hunting time or the impending darkness that's hanging low over the mountains in front of us.

I pull my hat over my ears and zip up my vest. It's cold enough where my ears are stinging and my chest feels hollow. It brings me back to late autumn field hockey practices and a wave of nostalgia washes over me. I smile quietly, remembering how we started all those years ago. I look up at Brian, he's sitting in the driver seat with the door open, patiently waiting for me to tell him I'm ready.

"Are you sure you're okay with this" I yell out for probably the tenth time since we parked. He turns and looks at me, eyes saying it all.

"YES. I want to do this and I know you need it. Stop asking me and just start." His curtness is ringing with love in my ears. Once again I'm reminded of how selfless he can be and again recommit myself to try to be more like him.

"Okay! Let's gooooooo!" The last word trails on as I start to kick my feet up and take the first few strides forward. Peace immediately washes over me. I haven't even moved a quarter of a mile and I'm set, fully content and filled with gratitude. The alpine lake sits quietly to my left. It's the deepest shade of seafoam green that I have ever seen. I keep moving forward, eyes glued to the water, counting the pieces of driftwood poking out near the shore.

I hear the soft roar of the car far behind me and the crunch of the gravel starts to get louder and louder. His voice breaks me from my trance.

"Go baby go baby go baby go! Yeaaah girl go 'head." I look over my shoulder and see him, window rolled down, smiling at me, inching very slowly along behind me.

That moment is sobering. And a little weird. But very, very satisfying. I keep moving forward, zig zagging around the divots and pointing out the potholes to him. The feeling is sitting in my chest and twinkling on my brain. We're in Washington, in the Olympics. I'm running and Brian is driving a snail's pace behind me because he doesn't want me to become cougar meal. And he's my husband. He's my husband and I'm his wife and he's wearing a snapback and a wedding band. We're in the mountains and he's happy. I'm running under towers of evergreens and bright yellow foliage, mountain range off in the distance. And I'm happy.

This feels too good to be true. Never in my fullest, quietest or wildest dreams did I think this could happen. Not because I didn't believe in us, but because I wasn't stupid. I knew what we'd put each other through. I was too familiar with the distance and pain and time apart.

I let that cliché wrap around me for a moment and decide it can stay. It exists for a reason and that reason is moving in this moment.

I stop for a minute to unzip my vest. In the past short miles I warmed up quickly. My hot skin felt stark against the crisp autumn evening air. But it wanted freedom from layers so I dumped the vest in the car.

"Girl you got way more in you. Keep going. We're not done." Brian looks squarely at me from the car.

"I know, I'm just taking, like, a second." I grin back at him. He really does look like a husband when he wears that hat.

I turn back towards the mountain and start running again. It's relatively flat so far and my turnover feels light and quick. My body is a bit achy from the drive that day and my mind feels zonked from everything in the past two weeks. But that's when I need it most. So I keep going, grateful to have that moment. We work our way around the curves and bends. Not a single car or person, or cougar for that matter, pass us. It's just us and the wild.

More miles pass and I can feel my body tiring. I don't want to push myself too far, knowing that rest is the best recovery. I stop abruptly at a pull-off and he pulls behind be.

"I feel like this is a good place to do it." He grins at me and puts the car in park, letting the engine cut off.

"I have mine on my phone but i think yours are in the trunk." While he walks to the back of the car I grab my flannel and jacket and throw them over my head. The sun has almost completely set, only a lick of purple remains stained in the sky, and the temperature has settled down.

I hear the thud of the trunk as he walks towards me and wraps his arms around my waist. I kiss his beard and stare at him, still feeling in awe but happy.

run wild & be

We walk to the edge of the cliff, the water twinkling below us and the mountains powerfully in front. He reaches into his pocket and slowly unfolds the paper. "Vows" is scribbled across the top of the page.

"Sydney…" He starts and it all goes perfectly still. My mind rushes to memorizes every detail of the moment. Listening to his deep voice read each line on the page. Watching his eyes move from my face back to the paper and up again. No matter how many times I tell myself it is happening I feel stuck in complete awe. Beautiful and endless awe that we are here forever.

132

every night

you fall asleep first
and i lay there
snug between your
hushed snores
and hot skin
wind tapping on
the worn pane
and then the dreamiest
sound, a mumbled
i love you
slips from your lips

when the growing grows up

i knew we could
stand and say forever
when i stopped looking
back, envious of what
old me had

break & build

i can see now
that we broke each
others hearts
over and over
so that now
i can vow
that when it
happens again
i will work
to build it back,
with endless care,
and know it will be
better than before

fleeting birthday thoughts

recently days have felt bittersweet,
at night i think about how i'll never get
that day back with you and so tomorrow
i will have to appreciate it even more.
then tomorrow comes and i think about how it could
never be better than today.

you and the range

sometimes i sit and stare at you
to make up for all the days
distance stole

the in between

her head hit the pillow,
body tired from the long run,
& when her eyes closed
an enormous smile cracked
across her freckled face.
the air was fresh -- a slight
reminder of roasted vegetables
still hung around from dinner.
his heavy arm draped over
her stomach, a decade's worth
of loving & fighting was carried
in its weight. so she sunk deeper
into the linen sheets & spent
the night steeping in the puddle
from her overflowing heart.

commit

you know the saying,
to know him is to fall in love with him when
you're fifteen and decide you want to
marry him when you're seventeen
and then do it seven years later

mt. st. helens

my favorite love
is made on the summit
in snow-capped stillness

ashford

my eyes open and there you are
squared between the A-frame
coffee cup in each hand
sleep in your eyes.
what a sweet place
to find a home

run wild & be

jars of honeymoon

mountains and
matrimony
suit him

142

cliffs of moher

i thought of you today
and I found us on a cliff
nothing blooms forever
but when it does
it's fooking ahhhmazing

143

bee

in his independent, grace-giving, honest, loving mind
i have found a home.

generational differences

they valued their time
not based on dollars earned
or money spent
but breathes taken outside
when bonfire breezes left
a trail of bumps along her skin,
in quiet moments with his
scratchy chest hair against her face,
and in cups of coffee run cold
while love made them full

endless

from the tips of telluride
and the pine lined road
going to the sun
the black cliffs down
into the canyon
you lay next to me
holding my hand
like back when there were
books, bleachers and jerseys

unconditional

you say you love my spirit
and i know, so
i keep your heart
tucked in the
spaces under my skin

ice cream dreams

it's sweetly sobering
when you realize things
you dreamt about for
six years
you're now living

run wild & be

rise, but don't forget to set

sometimes the sun needs a rest,
just like me.
see y'all,
we're not that different
after all

day/night

she dreams in
leafy greens
with dew dusted
slow sunrises and
her stride synced
to her paced pants

wild child mantra

a concoction to be
wildly & madly
in love with life :

rise & run
before the sun
then go again
after she sets
//

rest your body in
ice blue lakes
//

drink warm wine out
of camp mugs
//

fall asleep in the
backcountry
//

be unsure if it's
freckles or dirt
//

home

i sip my steamy cup of coffee
after our chilly morning run
and watch you cracking eggs
through the faded porch screen
as i walk down to the
weed-covered garden.
wildflowers haphazardly
but boldly zinging
up from the earth.
i let my toes wrinkle into
the soil and my heart
breathes out

day 1 of forever more

we woke up
with no plan.
just mugs of coffee
and a map.

rainier

you taught me that
purple mountains
can't always stain
a blue heart
but they can
drip peace through
their evergreen IVs

human home

her favorite part of his brain
is how it loves to grow
the best part of his heart
is that he's fought the conditioning
and you let it show
the greatest part of his spirit
is that it doesn't prescribe
to the human medication
of gender role

life goals

she learned very early
she needs very little & wants for even less.
just hours spent running
to heal her heart and make her feel complete,
like a puzzle piece.
then add big mountain peaks to bring her home
and make her feel whole.
and of course, through it all, his hand to hold, in the
happy & hollow moments.

run wild & be

ABOUT THE AUTHOR

/////

Sydney Zester, MPH is an advocate and creative who
believes in love, equity, long runs up big hills, and
community. She is driven to create a space where stories
about running, outdoors, activism, and creation can be shared
from the lens of a woman.

As a huge consumer of our outdoors she believes in
cultivating conversation around protections, conservation,
movement, and women within our mountains, deserts, and
oceans.

run wild & be

Made in the USA
Monee, IL
28 March 2020